PILGRIM · GUIDE

ST DAVID'S

Other titles in the Pilgrim Guide series

ST DAVID'S

Brendan O'Malley

Illustrated by
Shirley Norman

CANTERBURY
PRESS
Norwich

Text © Brendan O'Malley 1997
Illustrations © Shirley Norman 1997

First published in 1997 by The Canterbury Press Norwich
(a publishing imprint of Hymns Ancient & Modern Limited
a registered charity)
St Mary's Works, St Mary's Plain
Norwich, Norfolk NR3 3BH

British Library Cataloguing in Publication Data

A catalogue record for this book is available
from the British Library

ISBN 1-85311-168-6

Typeset, printed and bound in Great Britain by
The Lavenham Press Ltd,
Lavenham, Suffolk, CO10 9RN

Contents

I dedicate this book to the memory of my father,
Patrick O'Malley 1917–1996

Acknowledgements
I should like to thank Julie Trier of Trewellwell for her valuable assistance and advice and Beenie Phoenix for help in preparing this book for press.

Foreword

Where land stretches out to the Western Sea; where rock thrusts up to the sky; and where a little stream presses itself down into a sheltered valley: this is the place where David chose to come nearly a millennium and a half ago. He came to pray, and in praying gathered around him a small community who were the forerunners of those countless thousands who made the perilous journey by land and sea to this very special place. Many, like David himself, made this place the end of their pilgrimage and went journeying no more; many more took home with them the sense of the transcendent God and wove it into the texture of their spiritual lives.

It is this sense of the nearness of God in the tranquillity of the cathedral and its environs which still draws people here on pilgrimage. The very building and the sense of the numinous expressed within it; the bare, ruined chapels open to the sea and the sky have all inspired the writers quoted by Brendan O'Malley. He has woven their insights into the pattern of prayer and liturgy which he has created for the sites traditionally linked with the patron saint.

This book is meant to be used as you go around those sites and say your prayers in the footsteps of the saints. I commend it to your attention and to your devotions.

Wyn Evans
Dean and Precentor of St David's

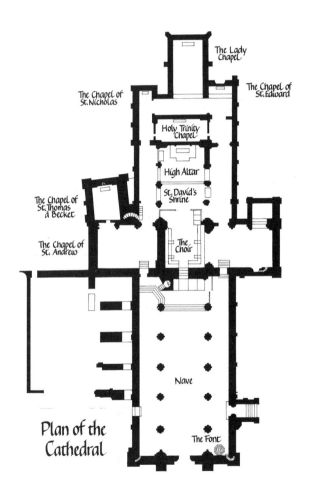

The Lady Chapel

The Chapel of St. Edward

The Chapel of St. Nicholas

Holy Trinity Chapel

High Altar

The Chapel of St. Thomas à Becket

St. David's Shrine

The Chapel of St. Andrew

The Choir

Nave

The Font

Plan of the Cathedral

How to Use this Book

In Part One of this *Pilgrim Guide* the Cathedral's numerous 'stations' or stopping-places are each described in turn, accompanied by some prayers and poems to help the pilgrim to focus on the stations' spiritual significance. Today's pilgrims may wish to begin their visit at the Font for the renewal of their baptismal vows. They could then continue with prayers at the other stations, culminating their pilgrimage at the Chapel of St Thomas à Becket (also known as the Chapel of the Blessed Sacrament). This approach is more in harmony with the Cathedral's sacred tradition than merely going round with a guide book in your hand!

In Part Two there are descriptions of the other sites of pilgrimage in the countryside surrounding St David's, accompanied by further prayers and poems to help the pilgrim on his or her spiritual journey.

de Leia built well, saw stone
vault and flower. A plain man,
building in faith where God
had touched the saint, he saw
the miracle which is not swift
visitation, nor an incredible
suspension of the commonplace
but the church grown great about us
as if the first stone
       were a seed

        Leslie Norris

Pilgrimage

St Augustine said, 'The soul finds rest nowhere until it rests in God.' Pilgrimage is an expression of this feeling and is essentially a search for God.

Pilgrimage seems to meet a profound human need to go beyond the limits of ordinary experience into the mysterious realm of the spiritual. Pilgrimage sites such as St David's seem to have the force of a spiritual magnet, attracting pilgrims into the depths of their life-giving mystery. Yet pilgrim places are not ends in themselves but serve as thresholds into new stages of life.

Pilgrimage to the Celtic fringes of Britain will invariably involve some discomfort, for the pilgrims travel through an often windswept elemental landscape which will test their endurance, perseverance and will to arrive at their destination. Inwardly they may also suffer as they leave old ways behind and strive towards a renewed spiritual life.

The poet Gerard Manley Hopkins coined the word 'inscape' to describe the inner nature of the journey which the pilgrim undertakes, and it too is often windswept and lonely. Pilgrimage fuses body and spirit into one: landscape and inscape merge into an experience where earthly life and the spiritual life intersect.

In medieval times pilgrims travelled to holy places to be near to those who would rise to glory at the Resurrection of the Dead. To come close to the grave of a saint was a special privilege, and great merit was attached to the custom of passing the night at a saint's grave. To rise with the saints on the Last Day was felt to be a form of 'spiritual life insurance' reserved for the worthy. Thus the shrine of a saint was an active source of spiritual energy. Although dead in the flesh, the saint was understood to be *there* – a formidable and powerful being who, if approached properly, would bring help to the suppliant.

When the early pilgrims travelled to Rome to see Peter's relics, their trip was to 'see Peter', not his bones. At a shrine pilgrims not only stood on holy ground, but entered holy time. At the sites where events in the life of Jesus took place, pilgrims saw beyond the archaeological remains and experienced the biblical presence, sharing in the reality of the events.

Pilgrims still flock to the old shrines for an infinite variety of reasons, yet all of them seem to agree with the earlier pilgrims that while God is everywhere, we sometimes need to seek him in special places. Human experience across the ages (and in our own age) shows us that certain places are more transparent than others, so that the divine presence may be experienced there more easily and tangibly. Those who, for whatever reason, hunger to see God's face will always beat a path to such places. Saint David's Cathedral is such a place.

PART ONE

SAINT DAVID'S CATHEDRAL

Saint David and His Cathedral

Remotely situated near the western extremity of Wales is St David's Cathedral, which equals any in the British Isles for beauty and interest, and is rivalled by only a very few. Its situation is unique: visitors, unless forewarned, would not know that it was there. They come first to the winding streets of the city of St David's, which is little more than a small town. Then, as they pass through an old gateway, there is spread out before them a valley and a scene of vast medieval splendour: a cathedral built from the local purple-coloured Caer Bwdy stone, harmonizing with the windswept natural surroundings. To the north lie the ruins of St Mary's College, and to the west, across the little River Alun, are the magnificent ruins of the Bishop's Palace.

This little city was once a place of considerable activity. St David, the patron saint of Wales, was held in such veneration that his shrine ranked with the holiest in the land as a place of pilgrimage. In fact, in medieval times two pilgrimages to St David's were counted as equal to one to Rome. But pilgrims were not by any means the only travellers to St David's, as the city lay on the old main road westward to Ireland. Among those who came were kings and nobles, who, having paid their reverence and made their offerings at the shrine, could rest awhile in the Bishop's Palace.

This remote corner of the British Isles became a place of pilgrimage purely as a result of the saintly reputation of David. His contemporaries called him Aquaticus ('the Waterman'), doubtless on account of his asceticism (he would allow no alcohol past his lips!) It is said in the ancient chronicles that his birth was miraculously foretold to St Patrick thirty years before the event.

The earliest life of David was written by Rhygyfarch, Bishop of St David's from 1088 to 1096. Legend tells that the Saint's parents were Sant, the son or grandson of Ceredig (from whom Cardigan takes its name), and Non, the daughter of Cynir and the granddaughter of King Brychan of Brecknock. David was born around the year 520. Legend says there was a great storm: his birthplace glistened as though the sun was visible and God had brought it in front of the clouds!

At his baptism at Porthclais David was held by a blind monk named Movi. A spring had burst from the ground at that place to supply the water for his baptism. Some of the water splashed into Movi's eyes, and he recovered his sight. The child was baptized by an accompanying Irish monk, Ailbe or Elvis, who later became Bishop of Munster.

The young David was brought up at Hen Fynyw (Old Menevia) and was educated by St Peulin (Paulinus) who also regained his sight through the intercession of his student. When his education was complete the newly ordained David set out on his travels, founding monastic settlements and churches. He is credited with the founding of twelve monasteries scattered as far apart as Glastonbury and Leominster. But his most important work was the establishment of the monastic foundation where now stands St David's Cathedral.

The monastery was founded in the face of fierce opposition from Boia, the chieftain of a local Irish settlement. He did his best to drive St David and his monks away, but eventually, through the prayer and example of David, Boia was converted to Christianity. He and his whole family were baptized.

The way of life at St David's monastery was similar to that

of the Egyptian Monasteries of the Desert Fathers, and although the regime was strict there was no shortage of recruits.

Tradition says that the death of David was foretold not only by himself, but also by a company of angels. It is generally accepted that he died in the year 589. His age at his death is unknown. His last words to his brethren were, 'Do the little things that you have heard and seen through me.'

St David's Cathedral

Eight hundred years the stones
Have borne attendance on Majesty
Here in this echoing House:
Stones from the cliff foot,
Wrought and hammered by a million years
Of sea and hurricane,
Cut and tooled in skilful pride
For vault and moulding.

Hallowed, time moved in them
As prayers ascended, and the rain
Beat its pattern
on the cloud-cold roof and aisles
Stripped of their covering
through the wanton years.

Eyes that measured time, and hands
honed by toil
Are irrecoverable dust;
And yet,
while this House stands
Not wholly can they die
who built it:

Within the stillness of a summer day
A shaft of sunlight will
with gold
Burnish afresh each shadowed arch,
Tracing its curve
as once
Some mason traced it with his
dreaming eye.
And it will stand afresh against the dark.
His living testament.

Mary Denyer[1]

Prayers at the beginning of a pilgrimage

O God, who required Abraham to leave his country and pre-served him safe and sound throughout his travels, grant to your children the same protection; uphold us in perils and lighten our journey; be unto us a shade against the sun, a covering against the rain and the cold; support us in our weariness and defend us against every danger; be unto us a staff to prevent falling and a port to welcome the ship-wrecked; so that, guided by you, we may attain our goal with certitude and may return home safe and sound. Amen.[2]

*

Loving God, whose glory outshines the sun, open our lives to the inspiration of your Holy Spirit that we may more fully reflect the glory of your love and share ourselves with one another in this time of pilgrimage. In Christ's name we pray. Amen.[3]

The Font

The Font may date back to the pre-Norman bishops, but the base cannot be earlier than the thirteenth century. Near it stands a very old font, possibly one of the most ancient relics in the Cathedral.

Baptism

The Christian life begins at baptism. Baptism is not an end in itself, but is part of our whole process of growth in spirituality. Pilgrimage may be seen as a 'Walking Retreat' when we seek to get into perspective the story of our life as a Christian. It is right and proper, therefore, to renew our commitment to Christ through the renewal of promises which may well have been made vicariously by someone else when we were too young to understand the nature of the commitment. Baptism, like the Eucharist, is a passage from the old to the new in which we die to all that has gone before and rise with Christ into newness of life.

As the Apostle Peter said, 'Repent and be baptized, every one of you, in the name of Jesus the Messiah; then your sins will be forgiven and you will receive the gift of the Holy Spirit. The promise is to you and your children and to all who are far away, to everyone whom the Lord our God may call' (Acts 2:38–40 REB).

What is your response to this promise? Pause for reflection.

Here at the Font (or perhaps before you come to the Cathedral) you may wish to renew your baptismal vows and/or to say the baptismal creed below:

A renewal of baptismal vows

Question: Do you renounce all evil influences and powers that rebel against God?
Answer: I renounce all evil.
Question: Do you trust in Christ's victory which brings forgiveness, freedom and life?
Answer: In faith I turn to Christ, my way, my truth, my life.

May God keep you in the way you have chosen.

A baptismal creed

I believe and trust in God the Father
who created all that is.
I believe and trust in His Son Jesus Christ
who redeemed mankind.
I believe and trust in His Holy Spirit
who gives life to the people of God.
I believe and trust in one God:
Father, Son and Holy Spirit. Amen.[4]

Prayer

Almighty God,
who anointed Jesus at His baptism
with the Holy Spirit
and revealed Him as your beloved Son,
we thank you for our fellowship
in the household of faith
with all who have been baptised in His Name;
keep us faithful to our baptism,
and so make us ready for that day
when the whole creation
shall be made perfect in your Son,
Our Saviour Jesus Christ.

The Nave

Traditionally the Nave had no seats and was for processions under cover. It is 130 feet long and is in the Transitional Norman or Early English style.

From the base of the Rood screen to the west door there is a slope of three feet. From the east wall of the Lady Chapel to the west wall of the Cathedral the ground slopes by fourteen feet (approximately the same height as the west door!)

Notice how the earthquake of 1248 caused the pillars at the west end of the Nave to lean outwards. During the 1600s and 1800s large buttresses were built to strengthen the nave's walls.

The rounded arches were built in 1180 by the Normans.

Within the stillness of a summer day
A shaft of sunlight will
with gold
Burnish afresh each shadowed
arch.
Tracing its curve
as once
Some mason traced it
with his
dreaming eye
And it will stand
afresh against
the dark
His living testament
Mary Denyer

Each has a different carved pattern. The windows have pointed arches. This style was popular when repairs were being made to the damage caused after the tower fell in 1220.

Prayers

Come, O Holy Spirit.
Fill the hearts of thy faithful
And kindle within them
The fire of Thy love.
Send forth thy Spirit
And they shall be created,
And thou shalt renew
The face of the earth.

*

God be in my head
And in my understanding.
God be in mine eyes
And in my looking.
God be in my mouth
And in my speaking.
God be in my heart
And in my thinking.
God be at mine end
And at my departing.

Sarum Primer (1558)[5]

The Cross

This modern Rood or hanging Cross shows Mary and John the Apostle beside the crucified Jesus. The original Rood stood above the pulpitum, where there was also a loft. The pulpitum has a central passage. There is skeleton vaulting inside the pulpitum decorated with mural paintings of the ascension of the soul into heaven and the crucifixion. On the ceiling are the names and symbols of the four evangelists.

Christ's Body

> Hands like these
> > Were hammered on the Tree:
> Feet like our feet
> > Were pierced: a head like our head
> Before the shameful thorns.

> What an honour, what joy it was, O Flesh,
> > To give the Son of God a body;
> A Jew's body at Bethlehem,
> > The mortal body of humanity:
> The Body that was transformed in the grave
> > into a living catholic Body.[6]

Prayer

Who in the passion of your blessed Son made an instrument of painful death to be for us the means of life and peace: Grant us so to glory in the cross of Christ that we may gladly suffer for His sake; Who is alive and reigns with you and the Holy Spirit, one God, now and for ever.[7]

The Choir

At its east end the Choir has a 'parclose' screen which makes it completely enclosed. Few other churches have screens like this. The stalls of the Canons of the Chapter lie in the Choir under the Tower. Note the medieval floor tiles. Some bear the coats of arms of noble families. Cromwell is said to have broken many of these when he rode up to the altar on his horse during the Civil War.

On the back of each Choir stall is painted the title or dignity of the Canon who sits there. The place-names are those of estates, manors or churches whose income supported that particular Canon.

Misericordia is a Latin word for 'pity'. Some seats here 'took pity' on clergymen who had to stand during long services. Note how they were able to rest their legs even when the seats were tipped up!

On one of the stalls is to be found the Royal Coat of Arms. St David's is unique among British cathedrals in that the reigning Sovereign is a member of the Chapter.

Prayers

Lord God Almighty, whose glory cherubim and seraphim and all the hosts of heaven with ceaseless voice proclaim, hear and accept, we humbly beseech thee, the praises of Thy Church below; and pour upon thy ministers in Choir and sanctuary such a spirit of faith, reverence, and joy, as shall lift both their hymns and lives unto thee, through Jesus Christ our Lord. Amen.

*

May David whose memory we devoutly celebrate on earth, unite us by his intercession to the angelic choir, God and our Lord Jesus Christ granting it, to whom is honour and glory throughout endless ages of ages. Amen.[8]

*

Hail to you, glorious Lord!
May church and chancel praise you,
May chancel and church praise you,
May plain and hillside praise you,
May the three springs praise you,
Two higher than the wind and one above the earth,
May darkness and light praise you,
May the cedar and sweet fruit-tree praise you.
Abraham praised you, the founder of faith,
May life everlasting praise you,
May the birds and the bees praise you,
May the stubble and the grass praise you.
Aaron and Moses praised you,
May male and female praise you,
May the seven days and the stars praise you,
May the lower and upper air praise you,
May books and letters praise you,
May the fish in the river praise you,
May thought and action praise you,
May the sand and the earth praise you,
May all the good things created praise you,
And I too shall praise you, Lord of glory,
Hail to you, glorious Lord![9]

The Shrine of Saint David

The Shrine of St David stands at the north side of the High Altar. Here, in a casket called a reliquary, were kept the saint's relics or remains. It once had a wooden canopy and panels painted with pictures of St David, St Patrick and St Denis of France.

Prayer

David, Christ's glorious Bishop, receive the desires of thy servants and intercede for us to our great Lord.

O God, who hast given to thy Church blessed David thy Bishop [as] a wonderful teacher: mercifully grant that we may deserve ever to have before thee this loving intercessor. Through Jesus Christ our Lord.[10]

LORD
teach us the silence
of humility.
The silence of wisdom.
The silence of love.
The silence that speaks
without words.
The silence of faith.
LORD, teach us to silence
our own hearts and minds
that we may listen to the
movement of the Holy Spirit
within us and feel your
presence in the depth
of our being
Amen

Pause for silence

Lord, teach us the silence of humility.
The silence of wisdom.
The silence of love.
The silence that speaks without words.
The silence of faith.
Lord, teach us to silence our own hearts and minds
that we may listen to the movement of the Holy Spirit
within us
and feel your presence in the depth of our being. Amen.[11]

The High Altar

At the centre of the Cathedral's worship of God is the High Altar, made in the shape of a table to remind us of the Last Supper. The present Altar is possibly smaller than the medieval one, which may have covered the whole of the top step. The area within the present altar rails retains its original tiles. Above the Altar is a window showing Jesus praying to God in the Garden of Gethsemane on the night of his arrest. The mosaics in the reredos are made from small pieces of stone or metal put together into a picture.

Prayers

God of infinite goodness,
from the very beginning of your Church
you have enabled her to renew her faith
through communion with the Body and
Blood of Christ.
May the sacrament of your love
sustain us as we journey towards the day
when this mystery will stand unveiled
for ever and ever.[12]

*

We commend unto thee, O Lord,
Our souls and bodies,
Our minds and our thoughts,
Our prayers and our hopes,
Our health and our work,
Our life and our death;
Our parents and brothers and sisters,
Our benefactors and friends,
Our neighbours, our countrymen,
And all Christian Folk
This day and always.

Lancelot Andrewes[13]

*

O God, your name is blessed from the rising of the sun to its setting; fill our hearts with knowledge of yourself and our mouths with your praise, that from East to West all may sing your glory, with one voice and with one accord, in Jesus Christ, your Son, our Lord. Amen.[14]

The Chapel of the Most Holy Trinity

In this Chapel, which is much visited by pilgrims, in the recess behind the High Altar, is an oak casket containing Holy Relics, thought to be the bones of St David and St Justinian.

The Chapel is noted for its fan vaulting. On the reredos behind the altar are the figures of St James, St Andrew, St Peter and St Paul. The Latin words on the reredos mean 'Behold the Lamb of God, who takes away the sins of the world.'

ECCE QUI TOLLIT
PECCATA
MUNDI
WHO TAKEST AWAY
THE SINS OF THE
WORLD

Prayer

The Three Who are over me,
The Three Who are below me,
The Three Who are above me here,
The Three Who are above me yonder;
The Three Who are in the earth,
The Three Who are in the air,
The Three Who are in the heaven,
The Three Who are in the great pouring sea.

Carmina Gadelica III 93[15]

Give us Life

Holy Spirit, Creator,
at the beginning you hovered over the waters;
you breathe life into all creatures;
without you every living creature dies and returns to
nothingness.
Come unto us, Holy Spirit.

Holy Spirit, Comforter,
by you we were born again as children of God;
you make us living temples of your presence.
Come unto us, Holy Spirit.

Holy Spirit, Lord and Giver of Life,
you are light, you bring us light;
you are goodness and the source of all goodness.
Come unto us, Holy Spirit.

Holy Spirit, Breath of life,
you sanctify and breathe life into the whole body of the
Church;
you dwell in each one of its members,
and will one day give new life to our mortal bodies.
Come unto us, Holy Spirit.

Taizé (adapted)[16]

The Chapel of Saint Edward

On the front of the altar are the first and last letters of the Greek alphabet, Alpha (A) and Omega (Ω). This is a reference to the Book of Revelation, where God says, 'I am the Alpha and the Omega, the Beginning and the End' (Revelation 21:6).

The altar was made from alabaster, which is not quite in keeping with the style of the rest of the building. The scenes carved above the altar depict the four beasts in Revelation chapter 4, and below them is a depiction of the New Jerusalem as described in Revelation chapter 7.

Lady Maidstone, the donor of the chapel, is buried on the left-hand side of the altar.

Prayers

All through its history, Lord our God, you have given your Church men and women of understanding, who have discerned the truth and shared it with their brothers and sisters. We ask you now, through the intercession of St Edward, to renew this grace in your Church today, that she may bear strong and faithful witness to you, in Christ, our Lord.

*

God of might and tenderness,
your Son underwent death to break its fetters.
Nothing can separate us from you.
Keep us ever in your love,
and so we will always be with those
whom you gave us,
and who have gone before us
to be with you.
This we ask through Jesus, our Lord.

The Lady Chapel

A Lady Chapel is one dedicated to the Blessed Virgin Mary, the mother of Jesus Christ. The construction of the Lady Chapel at St David's began in the late thirteenth century and was completed by Bishop Martin (d. 1328) as a five-bay vaulted structure. Bishop Gower added the tombs and the sedilia, and Bishop Vaughan remodelled the chapel completely as a two-bay perpendicular building. It lost its roof lead in the seventeenth century, but the vaulted ceiling did not collapse until 1775. The chapel was reconstructed by Aldred Scott at the beginning of the twentieth century.

Several of the original bosses (decorated blocks placed where the ribs of the vaulted roof meet) can still be found. There is a fine one of three hares sharing three ears (a symbol of the Trinity), and there is another one of a pelican feeding her young. When food is short a pelican will peck her breast and feed her children with her own blood, so the pelican has sometimes been used as a symbol representing Jesus Christ, who shed his own blood for us.

Prayers

Hail O Queen of heaven enthroned,
Hail by angels mistress owned.
Root of Jesse, gate of morn,
Whence the world's true light was born.
Glorious Virgin, joy to thee.
Loveliest whom in heaven they see.
Fairest thou, where all are fair,
Plead with Christ our sins to spare.

*

Pray for us, O holy Mother of God.
That we may be made worthy
of the promises of Christ.

*

O gracious and Holy Father, give us wisdom to perceive thee, intelligence to understand thee, diligence to seek thee, patience to wait for thee, eyes to behold thee, and a life to proclaim thee, a heart to meditate upon thee, through the power of the Spirit of Jesus Christ our Lord.

St Benedict[17]

The Chapel of Saint Nicholas

Saint Nicholas was the Bishop of Myra in Turkey. He is the patron saint of seafarers and pawnbrokers, but he is best known as the patron saint of children (Santa Claus is his Dutch name).

He gave three bags of gold as dowries to the three daughters of a poor nobleman so as to enable them to marry. Hence the pawnbrokers' sign.

Another story of St Nicholas tells of a wicked innkeeper and his wife who, having run out of food to feed their guests, resolved to murder three boys and make sausages with their remains. Just then St Nicholas called at the inn. The innkeeper was so conscience-stricken that he confessed all. The Saint restored the three boys to life.

A thanksgiving for children

He took a child, set him in front of them, and put his arms round him. 'Whoever receives a child like this in my name,' he said, 'receives me; and whoever receives me, receives not me but the One who sent me.'

(Mark 9:36–37 REB)

*

For the times when we have forgotten that children are our responsibility
to train and help and love.
Lord, forgive us.

For the times when we have not realized that our own growth is tied up
with what we do for children.
Lord, forgive us.

For the times when we reject children for their interfering with what we consider the real business of life.
Lord, forgive us.

For the times when we have been unaware of all that they can teach us
about relationship with God.
Lord, forgive us.

*

Let us put the needs of all children before you and ask your blessing on them and all who have dealings with children.

Help us to accept with understanding the teaching of the way of a child.

Keep children of all ages from evil – may there always be some grown man or woman to give them support.

Bless those who have no children of their own, that they may find joy in working in some way for them.

Keep us in our own homes alive to the riches that come to us from our children.

*

Almighty God, you use all creation to lead us to you. Let us learn from little children how to draw near to you, our Father in heaven. Amen.

The Chapel of Saint Andrew

Saint Andrew is the patron saint of Scotland and, like Jesus, was crucified. The shape of the cross on the flag of Scotland will tell you which way he was crucified. On the front of the altar in the Chapel of St Andrew can be seen the letters 'I.H.S.' They stand for the Latin words *Jesus Hominorum Salvator* or 'Jesus Saviour of Men'.

Prayers

Almighty God, who didst give such grace unto Thy holy Apostle Saint Andrew, that he readily obeyed the calling of Thy Son Jesus Christ, and followed him without delay: grant unto us all, that we, being called by Thy holy word, may forthwith give up ourselves obediently to fulfil Thy holy commandments; through the same Jesus Christ our Lord. Amen.

*

Remember all, who in their lives and by their deaths have borne witness to Jesus Christ in our Principality, and in this Cathedral.
Remember all, who are now preaching the Gospel of Christ, and are ministering the Sacraments.
Remember all, who day by day are seeking to confess Christ as their Master.
Pray that we may be strengthened by the Power of the Holy Spirit.
Pray that we may have the sense of the Divine Presence.
Pray that the Holy Angels may have us in their charge.
Pray for those who gave their lives in World Wars I and II.

Behold, I see the Heavens opened:
And the Son of man standing on the right hand of God.

*

Lead me from Death to Life
from Falsehood to Truth

Lead me from Despair to Hope
from Fear to Trust

Lead me from Hate to Love
from War to Peace

Let Peace fill our Heart

Peace Peace Peace

The Chapel of Saint Thomas à Becket (or the Chapel of the Blessed Sacrament)

Saint Thomas à Becket became Archbishop of Canterbury in 1162, but was murdered for his faith in 1170 after an argument with King Henry II. Miracles were said to have happened at his tomb. On a journey back from Ireland, King Henry once stopped at St David's to make penance for what he had done to Archbishop Becket.

This chapel has retained its fourteenth-century vaulted ceiling and is part of a three-storey building. Above it is the Cathedral Library, which is a medieval chapter house (a meeting-place for the Cathedral Canons); and above that is the Treasury, which is now the upper gallery.

Five roundels or bosses are to be found on the ceiling, including one depicting the Last Supper. There is also an

LORD JESUS:
YOU ALONE ARE THE FOOD
FOR ETERNITY
AND YOU ALONE,
YOU ALONE
CAN SATISFY
THE SOUL
OF MAN,
AND YOU
ALONE

ancient piscina (a hand-washing basin) on the right-hand side of the altar, with five early English carvings. It may well be that there was a chapel here shortly after the transfer of the body of St Thomas to the Corona, the shrine at Canterbury.

The chapel has an aumbry where the Blessed Sacrament is housed (hence it is also known as the Chapel of the Blessed Sacrament). A sanctuary lamp is lit to denote that the Communion bread, consecrated at the celebration of the Holy Eucharist, is present for the purpose of devotion and for taking Communion to the sick. The chapel is therefore specially set aside for private prayer, peace and silence.

Here are some prayers which will help you to focus on God in a time of peace and quiet in this chapel:

Prayers

Lord, I believe in you: increase my faith.
I trust in you: strengthen my trust.
I love you: let me love you more and more.
I am sorry for my sins: deepen my sorrow.

*

I worship you as my first beginning.
I long for you as my last end.
I praise you as my constant helper.
and call on you as my loving protector.

*

Guide me by your wisdom.
correct me with your justice,
comfort me with your mercy,
protect me with your power.

*

I want to do what you ask of me;
in the way you ask.
for as long as you ask,
because you ask it.

*

Let me love you, my Lord and my God,
and see myself as I really am:
a pilgrim in this world,
a Christian called to respect and love
all whose lives I touch,
those in authority over me
or those under my authority,
my friends and my enemies.

*

Help me conquer anger with gentleness,
greed by generosity,
apathy by fervour.
Help me to forget myself
and reach out towards others.

*

Thanks be to you, Lord Jesus Christ
for all the benefits which you have given me
for all the pains and insults which you have borne for me.
O most merciful redeemer, friend and brother
may I know you more clearly
love you more dearly
and follow you more nearly day by day. Amen.

PART TWO

OTHER LOCAL PLACES OF PILGRIMAGE

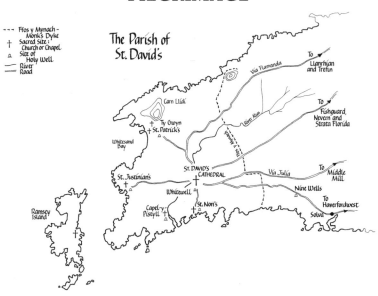

Map key:
- `- - -` Ffos y Mynach – Monk's Dyke
- `+` Sacred Site: Church or Chapel
- `Ω` Site of Holy Well
- River
- Road

The Parish of St. David's

Carn Llidi

+ Ty Gwyn
+ St. Patrick's

Whitesand Bay

Via Flamanda

River Alun

Ffordd y Saint

To Llanrhian and Trefin

To Fishguard, Nevern and Strata Florida

St. DAVID'S CATHEDRAL

Via Julia

To Middle Mill

St. Justinian's

Whitewell

Capel-y-Pistyll

+ St. Non's

Nine Wells

To Haverfordwest

Solva

Ramsey Island

Nine Wells (Naw Ffynnon)

In former centuries pilgrims approaching St David's from South and East Wales used to link with those from Devon, Cornwall and Brittany who had landed at Kidwelly near Carmarthen, to follow a common route westwards along the Via Julia. Resting perhaps at Clyn Ysbyty near Middle Mill (one of the many pilgrim hospices along the way), they would climb the steep hill into Whitchurch, where a large Calvary cross once stood, reflected in the village's Welsh name, 'Tregroes'.

Here, instead of making directly for St David's, sick pilgrims may have chosen to take *Y Llwbir Pererindod* ('The Pilgrim's Path') to Nine Wells to begin a round of visits to holy wells in the hope of a cure. The most accessible of the nine wells hides in an ivy-covered hood on a wide verge beside the main road.

After a healing ceremony the sick would be conveyed by cart (possibly taking refreshment at the Llandruidian hospice) to St Non's Well, half a mile south of St David's, where the cure would be completed. They were finally carried to the cathedral to be blessed by a priest.

Saints of Wales

Ye saints of Wales
by love of God led
with heavenly power incarnate.
Great ones entrusted with the leadership
of many Celtic peoples.

Ye, O David, Dragon –
Saint of the western shores;
Teilo mighty in the music
of the word.
Padarn, bearer of the staff of light
and Illtud of the healing bell.
Samson, Brynach, Dogwell, Dyfrig
of misty mountain, Holy Well;
pilgrims through earth, air, fire, and water,
seeking the love and power of God.

Flow within our hearts
and lighten our path
as we journey onward
through the shadows of the veil.

Blaise Gillespie

Saint Non's Chapel and Holy Well

Saint Non's Chapel marks the legendary birthplace of St David and is dedicated to his mother, St Non. The location may have been the site of a previous pagan shrine, for the remains of a Bronze Age stone circle surround the Chapel. Tradition says that, in order to relieve the agony of her labour pains, Non supported herself on a stone that lay near her, and afterwards it retained the prints of her fingers. It is said that when the Chapel was later built on that spot, this stone was introduced as an altar table.

Near the Chapel is the Holy Well of St Non, which (tradition says) sprang up at the birth of St David. The more likely explanation for the popularity of the well is that with the advent of Christianity, the worship of the gods and goddesses of the wells discontinued, but their places were taken by Christian saints such as St Non, to whom wells were then dedicated.

The sanctity of St Non's healing well has always drawn pilgrims aside on their journey to St David's. The sick were conveyed there in a cart from Nine Wells, and after their cure had been completed they were carried the final half mile to the Cathedral to be blessed by a priest.[18] The water of the well was believed to be efficacious for eye complaints and rheumatism.

The English antiquarian Browne Willis reported:

> There is a fine well … covered with a stone roof, and inclos'd within a wall, with Benches to sit upon round the well. Some old simple people go still to visit this Saint at some particular Times, especially upon St Nun's Day – which they keep holy, and offer pins, pebbles, etc. at this well.[19]

Another report expands upon this well's properties:

> There was so much faith attached to this once celebrated well that it was said every wish made there would be realized on making an offering and preserving silence. There is a traditional story of its virtues: it is said to have possessed the qualities of healing all complaints, but it was added there must be great faith … A person labouring under the heaviest affliction of lameness with difficulty attained the well upon his crutches; he immersed in this limpid stream and returned home with unspeakable joy, having left his crutches behind him at the well.[20]

Writing in 1811, Fenton noted that the 'fame this consecrated spring had obtained is incredible and still is resorted to for many complaints'.[21] At the side of the well was a place where pilgrims could place votive offerings.

In common with many other holy wells, St Non's Well was perhaps adopted as a baptismal focus during the Christian conversion of Western Europe, its latent spiritual properties transferred. During the early centuries people were baptized at wells, and later, water from the holy wells was carried to the fonts of churches for baptism, a practice that continued in some parts of Wales until the end of the nineteenth century.

The well-spring is a symbol of the basic source of life. Water is necessary for physical survival, let alone cleanliness, health and comfort; and it is necessary for baptism. The sacramental intermingling of the natural and the supernatural is very much in the Celtic Christian tradition. Water is not brought from somewhere and poured in a font; it is living water, springing forth from the ground. One may go down steps into the well – for, as may be found in many ancient baptisteries, baptism is both a cleansing and a going down into the death of Christ, and rising with him in new life. Holy Sprinkling is a natural sacramental action, when, by the use of water as a sign and pledge of God's grace, we are enabled to receive inward and spiritual healing.

Renewal of baptismal vows

Non's Chapel is a fitting place in which to renew one's baptismal vows.

*

Tremble, thou earth, at the presence of the Lord, who turned the hard rock into pools of water and the flint stone into a springing well.

Psalm 114:7–8

*

Let us pray: Lord, in your mercy give us living water, always springing up as a fountain of salvation: free us, body and soul, from every danger and admit us to your presence in purity of heart. Grant this through Christ our Lord. Amen.

(A period of silence may be kept for the examination of one's conscience.)

*

We thank you God for your love in all creation,
especially for your gift of water to
sustain, refresh and cleanse all life.
We thank you that through
the waters of baptism
you cleanse us,
renew us by your Spirit
and raise us to new life.
Through your Holy Spirit
fulfil once more your promises
in this water of rebirth,
set apart in the name of
our Lord Jesus Christ.

May praise and glory and wisdom,
thanksgiving and honour,
power and might,
be to our God for ever and ever.
Amen.

*

Water from the Holy Well is sprinkled on the pilgrim. The priest says:

May Almighty God, at the intercession of St David and St Non, grant us health and peace.

*

O Almighty God, you have knit together all of your people in one communion and fellowship in the mystical Body of your Son; grant us grace so to follow the Blessed St Non in good and virtuous living, that we may come to those unspeakable joys, which you have prepared for those who love you; through Jesus Christ our Lord. Amen.

*

May Almighty God bless us,
keep us from all evil
and lead us to eternal life. Amen.

Whitewell (Ffynnon Wen)

After miraculous cures had been effected at St Non's Well, the jubilant pilgrims would proceed towards their destination, the shrine of St David. Descending the path towards the sacred precincts, they would pass the Priory of Whytwel, a handsome building founded by Bishop Adam Beck in the late thirteenth century as a hospital for sick and infirm clergy. Pilgrims would be welcomed here to pray in the chapel or to drink 'water of the finest quality from the sainted spring of Whitewell'.

Close by, a triple basin beautifully carved from local purple sandstone has been discovered. The brothers at Whitewell may have washed the pilgrims' feet in this basin. This was called the Rite of Mandatum, which was a re-enactment of the washing of the Disciples' feet by Christ at the Last Supper. The Rite was a sign of humility and hospitality. The Mandatum basin may be seen at the St Non's Hotel nearby.

A footpath known as Pig's Foot Lane leads on towards the Cathedral Close. The name was derived from the 'Pyx', the portable Communion wafer box in which the Sacrament was carried.

Psalm 42

As a deer longs for the running brooks:
so longs my soul for you, O God.
My soul is thirsty for God, thirsty for the living God:
when shall I come and see his face?
My tears have been my food day and night:
while they ask me all day long 'Where now is your God?'
As I pour out my soul by myself, I remember this:
how I went to the house of the Mighty One, into
the temple God.
To the shouts and song of thanksgiving:

35

a multitude keeping high festival.
Why are you so full of heaviness, my soul:
and why so unquiet within me?
O put your trust in God:
for I will praise him yet, who is my deliverer and my God.
My soul is heavy within me:
therefore I will remember you from the land of Jordan,
from Mizar among the hills of Hermon.
Deep calls to deep in the roar of your waters:
all your waves and breakers have gone over me.
Surely the Lord will grant his loving mercy in the day-time:
and in the night his song will be with me,
a prayer to the God of my life.
I will say to God, my rock, 'Why have you forgotten me:
why must I go like a mourner because
the enemy oppresses me?'
Like a sword through my bones,
my enemies have mocked me:
while they ask me all day long 'Where now is your God?'
Why are you so full of heaviness, my soul:
and why so unquiet within me?
O put your trust in God:
for I will praise him yet, who is my deliverer and my God.
Glory be to the Father, and to the Son, and to the
Holy Spirit:
As it was in the beginning, is now, and ever shall be,
world without end. Amen.

The Revised Psalter

Nevern (Nanhyfer)

In this peaceful wooded valley, Brynach, an Irish missionary saint, founded his church within sight of the mountain, which he would often climb to pray in solitude. It is said that he communed with angels there – hence the name of the peak, Carn Ingli.

Like St David, his contemporary and friend, Brynach lived austerely, praying and fasting yet helping the poor. His sanctity was so renowned that many pilgrims would stop at Nevern on their way to St David's. Indeed, it was an accepted halting point, marking the beginning of the last stage of the pilgrimage. There is an old tradition that many travellers felt their strength failing here, after walking many miles over rough tracks, and that some died and were buried in the churchyard nearby.

Imprints show that they knelt to pray before the 'Pilgrims' Cross' carved into the rock-face on the path west of the church, and a set of worn steps, each with its own little cross, bears witness to the tread of countless feet. A dark tunnel of ancient yew trees leads towards the church. From one of these, known as the 'Bleeding Yew', drips a blood-red sap. Two sixth-century memorial stones, beside the church porch and built into a window-sill, bear both Latin and Ogham inscriptions, indicating the influential Irish presence at that time.

From the tenth century, pilgrims would have contemplated with awe the majestic 'Great Cross', which stands to the south of the church. Thirteen feet high, it is decorated with ribbon designs, an endless interlacing symbol of eternity. Upon the feast of St Brynach (7 April), according to legend, the cuckoo alights atop the Cross and sounds the first notes of Spring.

At Nevern

Nevern, signed with David's cross and Brynach's,
lay hushed and innocent. We stood
in the sunny churchyard. Tower and trees
rippled with heat-haze, as if a tiny breeze
passed over baptismal water
in a golden font. On Carn Ingli above,
Brynach walked with angels; the afternoon
was a pause in their conversation.
Silence surrounded the laughter of children
who broke from yew-trees' shadow
to run between the tombs.
Perception reached out to the hills
tentatively as a hand
to a loved face. Unborn words
were given into winged keeping.
In dusk on the northward road
we were too far away to hear
when at the carn the voices began again.

Ruth Bidgood[22]

Prayer to Saint Brynach

O Holy Brynach
who dared all things
to sail the ocean
and to live in blessed solitude.
Thou wast vouchsafed to see
wondrous things,
to spread the Gospel,
and to heal the sick.
Pray to God for us that we may
venture safely on the ocean of this life.

Eastern Orthodox prayer

Strata Florida (Ystrad Fflur)

One of the focal hospices on the route from North Wales to St David's was the abbey at Strata Florida. Originally a Norman foundation of the Cistercian Order, it was adopted by the conquering Welsh Lord, Rhys ap Gruffydd, and the building of the abbey began in 1184. It was to become a centre of medieval Welsh culture, where Welsh national chronicles were compiled and Welsh princes were brought for burial. The monastery flourished under the special patronage of Lord Rhys. It stood in a tranquil valley beside the River Teifi, the slopes of the Plynlimon mountains providing rich pasture for its sheep.

The Cistercian Order practised the rule of hospitality, by which guests were 'received as Christ himself'. Towards the end of the Middle Ages the poet Guto'r Glyn wrote, 'The abbey feeds many rich and poor.' Many bards were welcomed here, including the celebrated 'Bard of fair Glyn Teifi', Dafydd ap Gwilym, a contemporary of Chaucer.

At Strata Florida

This afternoon on the edge of autumn
our laughter feathers the quiet air
over tombs of princes. We idle
in an old nave, lightly approach
old altars. Our eyes, our hands
know fragments only; from these
the Abbey climbs and arches into the past.
We look up and find
only our own late August sky.

Ystrad Fflur, your shadows fall
benevolently still on your ancient lands
and on us too, who touch your stones
not without homage. Take our laughter
on your consenting altars,
and to the centuries borne up
by your broken pillars, add
the light weight of an hour
at the end of summer.

Ruth Bidgood[23]

Prayer to Our Patron Saints

In the steps of Christ
Brychan, Cledwyn, Teilo and David
did show us the way;
by their preaching they have
kindled the Light of the Gospel
in our land.
Be our guardian and our light,
O holy fathers of Wales,
pray for us.

Trefin

This cruciform village was once known as Trêfdyn. In medieval times it was a prosperous community and belonged to the Bishop of St David's. There was a grange farm (Long House) which was allotted 'two ploughs and sixteen sufficient oxen', and an episcopal manor, with large vaults beneath, built by Bishop Martin. Being only six miles from St David's, the manor served as an 'occasional residence of the bishops'. They frequently came here to get away from the busy life within the cathedral precinct and to breathe a purer air.

'The Black Book' of St David's states that in 1326 a fair was held in the village on the feast of St Martin (11 November). The south-bound pilgrims following the coastal route to St David's would have been fortunate to pass through Trefin on that day, as the women had baked their traditional mutton pies called 'pasteiod Ffair Fartin'. This would have been a severe temptation for those who were fasting during the

last few miles of their pilgrimage!

The road twists and plunges from Trefin towards Aberfelin, a rocky cove where, just above the shore, the ruined walls and idle quern-stones of a mill evoke images of past industry. A former Archdruid of Wales, Crwys, who was born in Trefin, immortalized the mill in his famous poem, 'Melin Trefin':

The Mill at Trefin

Tonight the mill is not grinding
At Trefin beside the shore,
The last pony, back burdened,
Has turned homewards from the door,
And the wheel that long since grated
And growled through the countryside
Had given its final turning
By the time the old miller died.

Beside the building's bare gables
The kindly stream runs still,
But the huge old wheel is not turning,
No barley is brought to the mill.
Where rough sacks of Llanrhiain's
Ripe wheat came at summer's end,
There is only a tress of seaweed,
And a few green rushes bend.

An idle stone is its guardian
In the pelting rain and the blast,
A memorial stone, unlettered,
Of the pleasant times now past;
But no one here is grinding,
Save slow time and weather unseen
Wearing away and grinding,
Grinding the mill at Trefin.

Crwys (1875–1968)[24]

43

Prayer

O Lord Jesus Christ, who art the way, the truth and the life: suffer us not we pray thee, to stray from thee, who art the way; nor to distrust thee, who art the truth; nor to rest in any other thing than thee, who art the life. Teach us by thy Holy Spirit what to believe, what to do, and wherein to take our rest. We ask it for thy Name's sake.

Erasmus (1467–1536)[25]

Preseli

The ancient track across the rounded hills of Preseli, was known as the Golden Way, since in Bronze Age times it was a trade route for Irish gold. It was also called 'Yr Hen Ffordd' (the old road) and 'The Pilgrims' Way'. It afforded another approach to St David's peninsula for pilgrims during the Middle Ages. They journeyed on foot, on horseback or by ox-cart, stopping occasionally at the chapels along the route. Two such pilgrim chapels probably stood in the tiny village of Mynachlog-ddu (Black Monastery). Its church belonged to the Benedictine priory of St Dogmaels. The foundations of a chapel remain at Croesfihangel (St Michael's Cross), two miles to the north, marking the way across the hills.

It was from Carn Meini, a rock outcrop along the spine of these hills, that the famous bluestone or spotted dolerite of Stonehenge was quarried at around 1700BC.

Sanctuaries

Yes, we saw the bluestones,
Ascending the mountain,
Sacred Preseli –
Up to the fountain

Of dappled dolerite
Bursting there,
Perpetually poised
On the waterblue air;

Stood, turned, and looked
            Down the long walls of Wales
                To where, beyond peaks
                And light-stippled vales,
                Under ultimate clouds
                The immortal rose
                Of holy Stonehenge
                Ever blows...

                                    Raymond Garlick[26]

Mountain Road

Sarn Helen traversed these flats and foothills,
        but we are heading for an older road.
    Almost as soon as there were men to walk it
the road was there across the plateau, falling giddily
        into valleys, clutching its way back up:
                narrow, uncompromising.

    Rain blurs the dingy green of winter fields,
    the distant patch of grey that is the town. Beyond,
        true hills begin, black today, magnified.
    Surely it is we who invent portentousness
            In earth's unmeaning bulk?

    Yet late in this clammy day, as we turn up
    into rainy wilderness, that thought falters.
        There comes a blurring of boundaries.
    All fought over, suffered, aspired to, loved –
here, there: then, now – seems one with what we write,
    this moment, on the barren hills' dark page,
        out of the depths of our uncharted minds;
    and what we feel now is the ancient awe.

                                    Ruth Bidgood[27]

Pilgrims' Prayers

Pilgrimage is not just about visiting places of spiritual significance. The whole of a Christian's lifetime is a pilgrimage – a continuous journey in which he or she is always searching for God and always travelling with God. Here are some prayers which speak about this life-long walk with God:

*

Love bade me welcome; yet my soul drew back,
     Guilty of dust and sin.
But quick-eyed Love, observing me grow slack
     From my first entrance in,
Drew nearer to me, sweetly questioning,
     If I lacked anything.
'A guest,' I answered, 'worthy to be here.'
     Love said, 'You shall be he.'
'I the unkind, ungrateful? Ah, my dear,
     l cannot look on thee.'
Love took my hand, and smiling did reply,
     'Who made the eyes but I?'
'Truth, Lord, but I have marred them; let my shame
     Go where it doth deserve.'
'And you know not,' says Love, 'who bore the blame?'
     'My dear, then I will serve.'
'You must sit down,' says Love, 'and taste my meat.'
     So I did sit and eat.

George Herbert (1593–1633)[28]

*

Dear Lord, Son of Mary,
     who trod the earth
     and shared our life
so that this fallen world might be restored:

Help us to
        walk in your way
        declare your truth
        and build your Kingdom in our land
By the power of your Spirit,
        and for your name's sake... Amen.

Author unknown

*

O God, help us to discern Your Truth in us. May our will be strengthened by Your Will; our love by Your Love, and our fragments of truth by Your Truth. Amen.[29]

*

God has created me to do him some definite service. He has committed some work to me which he has not committed to another. I have my mission – I may never know it in this life, but I will be told it in the next. I am a link in a chain, a bond of connection between persons. He has not created me for naught. I shall do good, I shall do his work. I shall be an angel of peace, a preacher of truth in my own place while not intending it – if I do but keep his commandments. Therefore I will trust him. Whatever, wherever I am. I can never be thrown away. If I am in sickness, my sickness may serve him; in perplexity, my perplexity may serve him; if I am in sorrow, my sorrow may serve him. He does nothing in vain. He knows what he is about. He may take away my friends, he may throw me among strangers. He may make me feel desolate, make my spirit sink, hide my future from me – still he knows what he is about.

Cardinal Newman[30]

References

Page ix   *At The Sea's Edge* © Leslie Norri's reproduced with permission

1.   From Brendan O'Malley, *Pilgrims' Manual: St David 's* (Paulinus Press, 1985)

2.   From Brendan O'Malley, *A Welsh Pilgrim's Manual* (Gomer Press, 1989)

3.   Ibid.

4.   From *An Alternative Order for Morning and Evening Prayer* (Church in Wales Publications, 1992)

5.   From *A Welsh Pilgrim's Manual*, op. cit.

6.   From D. Gwenallt Jones, *Gwreiddau* (Gomer Press, 1959)

7.   'The Feast of the Holy Cross' in *An Alternative Calendar: Lectionary and Collects* (Church in Wales Publications, 1995)

8.   Adapted from Rhygyfarch's *Life of Saint David*, concluding words of Section LXV, in *Pilgrims' Manual: St David's*, op. cit.

9.   Tenth- or eleventh-century Welsh, translated by Oliver Davies, from Oliver Davies and Fiona Bowie, *Celtic Christian Spirituality* (SPCK, 1995)

10.   From *The Life of St David* by Geraldus Cambrensis (c. 1146–1223)

11.   From *A Welsh Pilgrim's Manual*, op. cit.

12.   From *Proclaiming all your wonders: Prayers for a Pilgrim People* (Dominican Publications, 1991)

13.   From *A Welsh Pilgrim's Manual*, op. cit.

14.   Ibid.

15.   'Prayer to the Holy Trinity', *Carmina Gadelica* III 93 (Scottish Academic Press, Edinburgh)

16.   Teulu Duw, 'God's Family' (Council of Churches for Wales)

17.   From *A Welsh Pilgrim's Manual*, op. cit.

18.   Francis Jones, *The Holy Wells of Wales* (University of Wales Press, 1992) p. 26

19.   Browne Willis, 1716 *The Survey of The Cathedral Church of St Davids*, pp 52–3

20.   Manby, *History and Antiquities of the Parish of St Davids* (London 1801) pp. 56–7

21.   Fenton, 1811. *A Historical Tour Through Pembrokeshire*, republished by Dyfed County Council, 1994

22.   From *Collected Poems* (Seren Books, 1992)

23.   Ibid.

24.   From Joseph P. Clancy (trans.), *Twentieth Century Poems* (Gomer Press, 1982)

25.   From *A Welsh Pilgrim's Manual*, op. cit.

26.   From *Collected Poems* (Gomer Press, 1987)

27.   From *The Fluent Moment* (Seren Books, 1996)

28.   From *A Welsh Pilgrim's Manual*, op. cit.

29.   Ibid.

30.   Ibid.